LEADERSHIP

KEEPING IT SIMPLE

JODIE DAVEY

THE POWER WRITERS PUBLISHING GROUP

Published by The Power Writers Publishing Group in 2022.

Jodie Davey ©2022.

All Rights Reserved. No part of this book may be reproduced by any mechanical, photographic, or electronic processes, or in the form of a phonographic recording. Nor may be stored in a retrieval system, transmitted or otherwise be copied for public or private use other than for 'fair use' - as brief quotations embodied in articles and reviews, without prior written permission of the publisher.

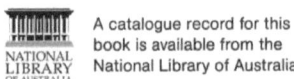

A catalogue record for this book is available from the National Library of Australia

ISBN 978-0-6451326-6-3

Disclaimer

Any opinions expressed in this work are exclusively those of the author and are not necessarily the views held or endorsed by others quoted throughout. All of the information, exercises and concepts contained within the publication are intended for general information only. The author does not take any responsibility for any choices that any individual or organisation may make with this information in the business, personal, financial, familial or other areas of life. If any individual or organisation does wish to implement the ideas discussed herein, it is recommended that they obtain their own independent advice specific to their circumstances.

The content of this book is general in nature, provides no individual clinical advice, and in no way replaces a medical consultation. Readers are advised to contact their own doctor or other health professional in relation to any clinical concerns they may have.

This book is available in print and ebook formats.

LEADERSHIP
Keeping It Simple
JODIE DAVEY

To my husband, Steve.
Your unconditional support, direct approach and honesty is what I needed in completing this book. When my confidence is down, you build it up. When I think big, you encourage and support my dreams and I am forever grateful.

To my mum, Helen.
For as long as I can remember you have been an inspiration. You are a true leader and I'm so blessed to have you as a mother and friend.

To the leaders in my life, past and present.
Each and every one of you have influenced my thoughts and actions.

To my editor and friend Kellie Nissen (Just Right Words). Thank you for being my guide and helping this dream come to fruition.

WHAT PEOPLE SAY ABOUT JODIE

Jodie's grasp of leadership is clearly demonstrated throughout this practical workbook. As Jodie infuses sound educational and leadership principles with professional and personal experiences, throughout the book, she exposes the qualities required for effective leaders. Using the LEADERSHIP acronym Jodie guides the reader through fundamental yet practical steps and hints to refine or develop their leadership skills. Whether already in leadership positions or emerging, Jodie indicates in, Leadership: Keeping it Simple, we are all leaders. What Jodie does is makes leadership accessible and easy to be a leader!
Dr Lynette Stockhausen (DipT, BEd, MEdSt, PhD)

A well-written thought-provoking book which helps teachers to explore and expand their leadership skills within the Education sector. Jodie's wealth of experience in this space is evident in the practical examples that she provides. It is a book for all educators, not just those who are currently in leadership positions but anyone who is keen to develop their skills within their position.
Dannielle Charge (BPsych) – Director of Thrive for Teachers

This book takes the complexity of leadership and explains it with refreshing simplicity without losing any of the substance.
Rachel Wicks (BComms, Grad Cert Pub Pol, MEval) – Coordinator Community and Social Resilience, Cairns Regional Council

EDITOR'S NOTE

The story of how I met Jodie Davey and came to be lucky enough to edit her first book is a long one that I will try my best to summarise.

In a nutshell, I used to be a teacher and had enrolled in Jodie's *Coaching /Mentoring* course along with a few colleagues from my school. However, I was there with an ulterior motive – one that I suddenly found myself sharing during the opening introductions.

"Hi. I'm Kellie. I probably shouldn't be saying this but I'm here under false pretences because I'm on my way out of teaching and have started running my own editing and book coaching business. I know this course is targeted at teachers but I'm pretty sure I'll gain plenty of insights for my book coaching as well."

Jodie's response floored me. "We need to talk during the break," she said. "I'm writing a book."

The rest is history and the result is this wonderful book, *Leadership: Keeping it Simple*.

One of the many things I love about Jodie is that she is genuine. She walks her talk and says things as they are. If you have attended any of her courses or have heard her speak elsewhere, you will 'hear' her voice as you read this book. She is authentic and down-to-earth, and she knows her stuff.

Leadership: Keeping it Simple is THE book for teachers who are aspiring leaders or who are already school leaders and looking to improve and grow. However, if you aren't a teacher, I challenge you to NOT find words of wisdom, advice and strategies in these pages that you can apply to whatever role you undertake in your life.

Enjoy the journey.

Kellie Nissan – Founder of *Just Write Words*

ABOUT THE AUTHOR

I began my teaching career in 1992 as an enthusiastic 20-year-old. For my first role, I was posted to a country town in South Australia. I spent four years teaching in primary schools in this region and absolutely loved it. Teaching was never really a profession I had considered during high school and yet here I was – excited, passionate and fulfilled. I truly believed I was making a difference to my students every day. The classroom was where I wanted to be.

In my fifth year of teaching, I was posted to a city school as a Curriculum Leader. This was my first taste of leadership. After six months, I was asked to act in the Deputy Principal role for the remainder of the year.

I was up for the challenge but I quickly realised I knew very little about influencing others. I didn't know the difference between managing and leading. I didn't know how to empower others and bring out the best in them. I felt a little overwhelmed and out of my depth but I wanted to learn, grow and develop as a leader. What I needed was a simple 'playbook' to get me started and I vowed that, one day, I would help other leaders navigate the complexities of leadership in a simple way.

I continued classroom teaching for several years. I taught in international schools, the Catholic sector, state schools and independent schools, experiencing both primary and secondary settings. With every role, my teaching practice grew. Although I stepped into a number of leadership roles along the way, my heart was always in the classroom. I was having an impact on thirty students and I was proud of this.

One day, out of nowhere, I saw leadership differently. Instead of viewing leadership as 'sacrificing my love of the classroom', I saw it as an opportunity to make a difference to MORE students. It was an opportunity to impact and influence teachers, who, in turn, would impact and influence their students. This was my lightbulb moment. I knew I was ready to leave the classroom and become the leader I would follow.

I spent the next twelve years of my career in various leadership roles – Assistant Principal, Curriculum Adviser, Director of Teacher Performance and Development and now, thirty years after walking into my first classroom as a beginning teacher, an Education Consultant managing my own business, Powerful Partnerships.

I still hold students at the centre of all I do and I adore working with other educators and leaders. I look forward to continuing this important work into the future.

To find out more about Jodie Davey and the courses she offers through Powerful Partnerships, visit her website
https://www.powerfulpartnerships.com.au/
or contact Jodie directly at
jodie@powerfulpartnerships.com.au

ABOUT THIS BOOK

There is leadership potential in all of us and I want to help teachers unlock that potential.

This desire is why I created my *Leadership* program – a one-day course designed for teachers who want to develop their leadership qualities and for current school leaders who are looking to improve.

The course is one of my most popular but participants keep asking, "Do you have a book?"

"I have a workbook," I say.

"Which is great, but it's not the same as a book."

Teachers love books. And now I've written one.

Leadership: Keeping it Simple is my course and my experience in hard copy. It is a book you can pop in your bag and dip into whenever you need inspiration or reassurance that you're doing okay.

There is no 'perfect' way to lead. There are many different types of leaders, each with attributes that appeal to some and not others. Multiple contexts are at play, each one requiring different leadership actions.

This book will not give you definitive answers on how to be an effective leader but it will get you thinking about the leader you want to be.

In the following chapters, you will find practical ideas, real-life situations and useful tips to help you become the best leader you can be. To get the most out of this book, I would encourage you to not just read it, but to actually stop wherever I pose a question and reflect. Especially where you see the Powerful Partnerships symbol. I say this because I haven't just written this book for you to learn about leadership. I've written it to help you step into your leadership potential. The act of stopping to consolidate what you've read by reflecting on exactly how it relates to where you are right now will help you to get to where you want to be.

I hope the words in this book resonate with you, wherever you may be on your leadership journey. I hope they give you reminders about where to focus your time and energy and that you are inspired to continually strive to be the best leader you can be.

My intention is to provide a book you can refer to regularly as your journey evolves and that will become a useful tool in your leadership kit.

We are all leaders.

Throughout our leadership journey, we must all ask ourselves this question:

What is it like to be led by me?

Become the leader you would follow.

Good luck with your future endeavours.

CONTENTS

What Is Leadership?	xv
CHAPTER ONE	1
Have A Plan	
What is it like to be led by you?	1
What is your vision?	2
What are your values?	3
CHAPTER TWO	7
Listen	
Why listen?	8
Listen, don't solve	9
Delve a little deeper.	9
It's not about the nail	11
Are you a good listener?	12
CHAPTER THREE	15
Emotional Intelligence	
Hint 1: Watch the walk	16
Hint 2: Read body language	17
Hint 3: Avoid defensiveness	18
Hint 4: Be proactive	18
Hint 5: Get to know your staff	19
CHAPTER FOUR	23
Affirm	
Public or private?	26
CHAPTER FIVE	29
Deliver	
Under-promise and over-deliver	30
CHAPTER SIX	35
Everyone	
How does everyone have the capacity to be an effective leader?	36

CHAPTER SEVEN *Relationships*	41
Hint 1: Be fair with everyone	41
Hint 2: Take care not to damage relationships	42
Hint 3: Maintain a professional distance	42
Hint 4: Be open and transparent	43
Hint 5: Work on developing relationships with everyone	43
Establishing the relationship	44
Developing the relationship	44
Maintaining the relationship	44
CHAPTER EIGHT *Support*	47
Hint 1: Clear policies and procedures	47
Hint 2: Focus on being effective	48
Hint 3: Support teams	48
Hint 4: Develop mentoring and induction programs for all staff	49
CHAPTER NINE *Humility*	53
CHAPTER 10 *Integrity*	57
How do we build and maintain trust?	58
CHAPTER ELEVEN *Presence*	61
CHAPTER TWELVE *The Best Leader You Can Be*	67
References	71

WHAT IS LEADERSHIP?

WHAT WORDS CONVEY 'LEADER' TO YOU?

We often use the term 'leadership' as if it is something we have to get into.

"I want to **get into** leadership."

or

"How do I **get into** leadership?"

If I asked you to think of some words that depict a leader, you could probably come up with hundreds of applicable ones.

What words convey 'leader' to you?

Inspiring. Motivating. Communicator. Passionate. Visionary. Respected. Honest. Integrity. What else?

There is no doubt these are all desirable leadership qualities but is it possible to be all of these things, all the time, to all involved?

When I consider the list of qualities I believe a good leader needs, I want to run far away from any leadership opportunities. Being a leader is hard. How can I live up to my own expectations?

Instead of listing leadership qualities, think about a leader you admire. This can be someone you have worked with or for in the past. Or this person may be a social acquaintance. Ask yourself: Why do I admire this person as a leader? Considering leadership in this way is less confronting and more personal.

Whenever I consider this question, my response always comes back to how the leader made me feel, the potential they saw in me, how they guided and nurtured me and the respect they showed me. I want to be like them. The leaders I admire were inspirational and motivating. Each one had great communication and integrity. They all had 'leadership qualities' but when I narrow these down, the reasons I admire them are all about me.

They motivated **me**.

They trusted **me**.

They gave **me** opportunities.

Leadership is not jargon, nor is it a word that can be easily defined.

Leadership is about the impact and influence our actions have on those we are leading.

Ask yourself this question: What is it like to be led by me?

Before you answer, consider **your** influence on others and reflect on **your** impact.

Being an effective leader is all about impact.

Leadership is complex. As humans, we have a tendency to overcomplicate many things in our lives and leadership is no different. I want to help you look at leadership in its simplicity. To focus on the things we can control and the differences we can make in the lives of others through our actions. It doesn't need to be complicated. Quite the contrary, it can be very simple.

CHAPTER ONE

HAVE A PLAN

Do you see yourself as a leader? Are you an effective leader? Sometimes we confuse leadership with the role we are in. We assume those in positions of responsibility are leaders but may not look at ourselves as leaders. Leadership doesn't just come in the form of CEOs and Principals. If you manage a soccer team, you are leading. If you're a parent, you are leading. If you teach, you are leading. Leadership is about the impact and influence you have on others, not about the role or title you hold.

The ability to reflect on your impact, which is the essence of effective leadership, will help you continue to grow and develop your skills.

WHAT IS IT LIKE TO BE LED BY YOU?

Asking yourself this question is the most powerful self-development tool and allows you to discover areas where you are successful as well as those needing further work. Regardless of your role, it is critical you determine your impact by stepping into the shoes of the people you lead and seeing yourself as they see you.

As you think about this question, it is important to avoid 'blaming thoughts':

- I have reluctant staff.
- That member of the team is difficult.
- Nothing will get through to that person.

Blaming thoughts create the illusion it's not your leadership that is the problem. There will always be enablers and there will always be those who are less likely to 'jump on board' early, but focus the lens back on yourself. Ask what you can do differently to overcome obstacles and achieve the outcomes you are after.

Be is a powerful word when I'm trying to reframe my thoughts.

- I will **be** more patient.
- I will **be** more understanding.
- I will **be** a better listener.

Using 'be' prevents me from blaming others and making excuses. It sets me a challenge to take control where I can and do something about it.

WHAT IS YOUR VISION?

In your role as a leader, it is crucial to have a vision and share it with your colleagues.

Your vision needs to reflect your goals and clearly define the direction you intend to take. It should also be synonymous with the culture you want to establish. Understanding the current culture is critical as it will assist your planning for future improvement.

Developing a holistic acceptance of your vision will allow you the best opportunity for success as your team works with you to accomplish your organisational goals.

What is the vision of your school?
What is your vision as a leader?

You want these to align.

New principals are often faced with taking over the vision already in place. This requires confident leadership and patience. As a leader, you need the vision for your school to align with your vision or coherence is lost. However, it may not be wise to change the school's vision in your first week. Be patient, assess the current culture and plan for change diplomatically.

Remember that the strategic plan you develop is a working document and must consider all facets of your school. Be mindful of the ever-changing nature of education and ensure you have flexibility within your plan to accommodate these changes.

As you read this book, you may find it useful to note down some reflections. This can be a powerful tool, not only now but later when you look back at your earlier thoughts, determine your growth and reassess your direction.

WHAT ARE YOUR VALUES?

The values you model as a leader will ultimately define your organisation. The way you behave is a direct result of what you believe, and the experience you give and receive in any situation is a direct result of the way you behave.

For example, if I believe in caring for the environment, my behaviour is to place rubbish in the bin. The experience I receive and give to others is a cleaner place to live.

As a leader, if I believe in honesty, the behaviours you will see may include open feedback, addressing issues face-to-face and having difficult conversations when required. The experiences for all are likely to include greater performance growth, stronger unity and less conflict.

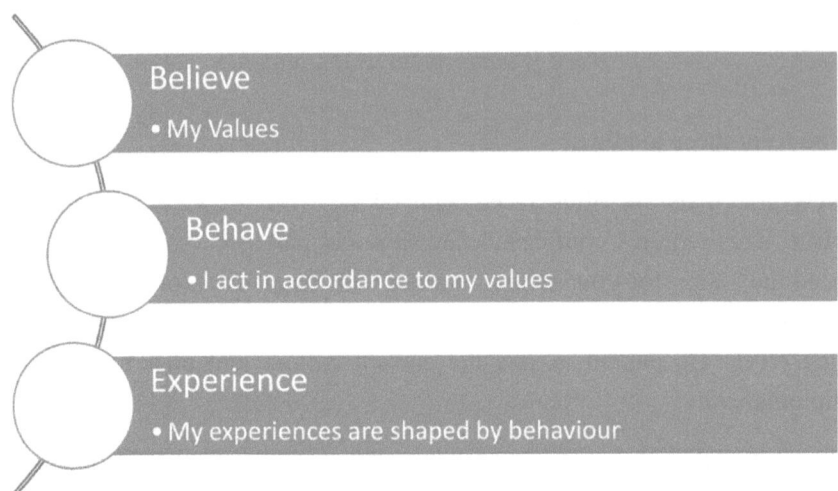

Being very clear about what you value helps to maintain integrity and consistency in behaviour. In turn, this leads to a greater sense of trust within your team. Share your values with your staff and publicise them through meeting agendas, staff noticeboards and any other medium you use.

Your staff are your greatest asset. They need to be valued, respected and cared for, and they must be engaged in your strategic plan. See the best in every individual and listen to their needs, ideas and issues. Lead them in the way you like to be led. Support and guide them to help create the culture you desire.

The following chapters explore some key traits and actions required for leaders to be successful. I use the LEADERSHIP acronym to help you remember the key words so you can adopt them as part of your day-to-day work. Some are character traits you may naturally exhibit. Others are ones you may need to develop with conscious effort. The remainder are actions important to your development as a leader.

OVER TO YOU

HAVE A PLAN

Reflect on the leaders you know – not only the ones you respect but also the ones you feel may have been able to do better. Working with a range of leaders gives us opportunities to learn and grow into the leader we want to become. Use all experiences as opportunities to reflect and develop.

Before you begin working through the LEADERSHIP acronym;

L – Listen
E – Emotional Intelligence
A – Affirm
D – Deliver
E – Everyone
R – Relationships
S – Support
H - Humility
I – Integrity
P - Presence

Consider the type of leader you already are and the one you want to become.

- What qualities are important to you?
- Where do your strengths lie?

- What areas do you want to work on?
- Are you open to improvement and reflective in your ability to lead others?
- Where are your support networks and how can you harness the gifts of others to help you evolve?

Always remember:

Be the leader you would follow.

CHAPTER TWO

LISTEN

Lists en with your ears, eyes, body and heart. No matter how much work is waiting for you back in your office, listen completely and genuinely.

The power of listening; I cannot emphasise it enough.

Taking a silent walk around your school will give you so much information if you consciously listen to the general chatter, the day-to-day school noises and the tone of conversations between children, parents and staff. What vibe do you sense? Happy, productive and valued? Or overworked, tired and frustrated? Do the sounds you hear change according to the time of day or the time of year? Be mindful as you listen. You will notice so much when you put your mind to it.

Listen with your ears, eyes, body and heart

Each day, take a few minutes to listen. Note down what you hear and trust the feelings you get as you listen.

WHY LISTEN?

By consciously listening, we can begin to gather insights into the well-being of our staff and how they are tracking.

We do not need to solve all their problems or answer every query. As humans, our instinct is to want to 'save' others. Fixing problems for our colleagues makes us feel worthy and helpful, however, in doing so we take away the opportunity to equip them with the skills they need to solve problems for themselves. We are actually creating more work for ourselves and acting as the problem-solver may lead to dependency and an expectation that all issues will be magically fixed once they land on the leadership team's agenda.

By genuinely listening to our staff and setting aside time to discuss their issues with a solution-focused mindset, we will fill their capacity, avoid additional work for the leaders and build a team of empowered teachers who are solution-focused and add value to the school.

A problem without an alternative solution is just a whinge.

This phrase, which I unashamedly stole from Theodore Roosevelt, took pride of place in my office during my time as an Assistant Principal. Even today, it reminds me that effective leadership is about empowering others, not about fixing problems and feeling good about myself.

Listen to all sides, there is always more than one

Stephen Covey, author of *The 7 Habits of Highly Effective People* (2004), reminds us that our role as leaders is to listen to understand, not to reply. By listening to understand, we aim to get the best out of others and support them in achieving more than they thought they could. Whether you are listening to the ideas of your team, their challenges or their successes, an effective leader asks the right questions to help clarify the issues and solutions. Setting norms around listening to understand, and helping your staff bring a positive mindset to meetings and discussions are crucial steps towards empowering others to build their capacity.

LISTEN, DON'T SOLVE

Consider the following scenario:

> *A colleague shares with you some challenges they are facing with a particular student in their class. They describe the behaviours and the strategies that don't seem to be working. They use comments like "I always get the tough students" and "There's no support".*

Have you been in a similar situation? Did you listen to understand or were you thinking about what you were going to say next, in order to solve the issues for them?

In these situations, many of us just want to fix the problem. I encourage you to avoid this and simply listen. Listening is powerful, yet because we are so busy, we often get caught up in the solutions. Ultimately, we want others to solve their own problems through our guidance and leadership. Jumping in with the answer won't help. Stop, take a deep breath and just listen.

Individuals are complex! Everyone has varying perspectives and we all see issues differently depending on where we stand.

DELVE A LITTLE DEEPER.

When staff come to you with an issue, consider asking questions such as:

- How long has this been an issue?
- What action have you already taken?
- What outcome are you looking for?
- What is the best way to move forward?

- How would you like me to be involved?

These questions not only help us clarify the details of the problem, but they also guide our staff in coming up with potential solutions themselves.

Expanding our understanding along multiple perspectives is essential as a leader. Listening to different points of view, ideas and creative insights improves our likelihood of success when it comes to achieving our goals and bringing our school's vision to life.

All stakeholders within the school community have something to contribute. Our success is defined by our ability to listen first and then determine which information to act upon and which to filter. Important conversations can be driven underground if we don't listen in the first instance or when we don't establish an appropriate forum for staff to have their say. The staffroom will soon become the venting area, effectively diminishing the culture you are trying to establish.

In summary:

- Focus on what's being said.
- Free your mind of your own thoughts.
- Allow yourself to hear the thoughts of others.
- Filter later.

Making connections is an important part of the process for establishing, developing and maintaining relationships. However, in our attempt to find common ground or a connection, we often jump in too early with our responses and fail to really listen. Be mindful of this tendency.

The following personal example of the first time I truly appreciated the power of listening is the best way I can show what I mean.

My husband and I had been undergoing IVF treatment for a short while. Unless you have been through this experience yourself, it is very difficult to really understand the complex emotions that go hand in hand with trying to have a child. It's not in my nature to share every intimate detail with anyone who passes by but in talking about some aspects of the process with a few friends and colleagues, I came to truly appreciate the art of listening.

*Many people I talked to fell into one of two groups: connectors or fixers. The **connectors** would reply quickly in their attempt to make connections and build relationships. "My friend went through IVF" or "My sister's neighbour's cousin's daughter had IVF" were comments I heard more than once. While I completely understood the intention was to connect, their comments failed to help them truly understand.*

*On the other side, the **fixers** would listen but were then compelled to give solutions. "You just need to relax", "You should just stop trying" or "I heard you should drink more tea". Once again, their intent was to help but advice was not necessarily what I was looking for.*

I just wanted people to listen with the intent to understand and there were many who were able to do this. They asked questions like "How are you coping?", "Would you like to chat further?" and "Is there anything I can do?"

Questions show a person is listening and understanding. Questions also show incredible leadership, whether it's from a personal connection or a professional one. This is the behaviour of an effective listener.

Consider a time when you had a colleague come to you to share something. Did you use effective 'listening to understand' strategies or were you a connector or a fixer? For many educators, our natural disposition is to provide solutions for others. It's often a hard habit to break but being mindful of your listening techniques can go a long way towards helping you further develop your listening skills.

IT'S NOT ABOUT THE NAIL

This is the title of a fabulous clip you can find on YouTube. It highlights the difficulty we have in holding back the need to fix, especially when the solution is glaringly obvious. And it will give you a laugh as a bonus.

Listen to be challenged and you will learn something new

We are all busy. However, if we allow ourselves to be too busy to listen, we'll miss valuable insights into how our colleagues are feeling and will miss the ideas they have to share.

One of the most overlooked aspects of listening is thanking contributors for their thoughts and ideas. We do not have to agree with them but acknowledging all contributions is essential. A simple acknowledgement encourages people to continue contributing. Not only will they feel valued but your school community will reap the long-term benefits of open communication and multiple perspectives.

All members of your school community should feel empowered to speak with the knowledge they will be listened to by good leaders. Regardless of their role or title, individuals add to the worth of our school by offering different perspectives.

A few years ago, an issue arose in relation to playground safety in a school where I was working. Many people were consulted, including parents, teachers, administrators and students. Everyone, that is, except the most important person – the groundsman. In the end, it turned out he actually had the best solution.

Great insights can be had by anyone, regardless of their role.

ARE YOU A GOOD LISTENER?

It is worth asking trusted friends or colleagues to give you an honest answer to this question. Make sure you identify your listening strengths as well as your weaknesses, and then use these insights to commit to continuing to listen effectively and to work on the areas that need improvement.

Everyone can grow their ability to truly listen.

OVER TO YOU

LISTEN

Never underestimate the power of truly **listening**.

Consciously consider what you hear and then determine your actions based on this. Try not to automatically assume someone is looking for a solution when they speak to you. Listen, consider, develop a better understanding through your questioning and then determine how you can assist others to solve their problems themselves rather than relying on you to be the fixer.

- Are you present when you're listening? How do you know?
- What are three things you can do to improve your ability to listen? Make a note of these and start working on them.
- Consider the leaders you admire. Are they effective listeners?
- How do effective listeners demonstrate their ability to listen?

CHAPTER THREE

EMOTIONAL INTELLIGENCE

Once words are spoken they can do harm in a flash. There is no turning back. Our ability to use non-verbal cues, such as body language and tone of voice, helps us read situations and gather information about the wellbeing of our staff. In turn, this information guides us in what we say and when we say it.

I always thought emotional intelligence – often referred to as EQ – was common sense. Reading people is something I find relatively easy as I am always conscious of the state of mind of those around me. It wasn't until I worked with someone who was in a leadership position that I realised EQ is not common sense for everyone. Being able to read subtle cues – body language, tone of voice, stance, eyes – and being able to process some meaning from these cues gives you a greater opportunity to say the right thing at the right time. Even better, you can avoid saying the wrong thing at the wrong time! However, your EQ is more than just reading the emotions of others; it's about being aware of your own emotions and what these might look like to others.

Try not to have your 'I can't believe you just said that' face on during a meeting and avoid your 'are you seriously complaining again?' face when someone is sharing a concern. As leaders, we must be open to everyone by listening with purpose and without judgement. It is important to monitor your emotions so as not to give the wrong impression.

You must seek to understand your staff

If reading people doesn't come easily to you, I urge you to do something about it. Learn how to interpret cues and understand the people around you because this skill is crucial to your leadership future. Understanding your staff will help you know when they need you to be caring and gentle and when you can push them a little further.

Here are a few practical hints that have helped me.

HINT 1: WATCH THE WALK

Watch the way your colleagues walk from their car to their workspace. Is there a skip in their step? Do they walk with purpose and intent? Are they smiling and greeting people along the way? Do they look energised?

These simple observations can provide insight into an individual's current state of mind. A person who exhibits the above characteristics is likely to be a productive contributor, engage well with parents, communicate effectively with colleagues and positively influence their students.

Do your staff show positivity in their walk?

On the other hand, if you notice people moving slowly, shuffling their feet with their head down and ignoring others as they walk inside, something is amiss. There may have been a drama at home. Maybe a personal matter or a health issue is worrying them. It could be financial or relationship stress. Or perhaps they are feeling pressured or undervalued in the workplace.

Rushing, looking frazzled, trying to do multiple things at once or having no poise in their walk are also indicators something is not quite in sync.

Any person displaying one of the latter two characteristics is not going to be positive and productive in your workplace unless you are there to support them.

When we take time to observe this morning behaviour, we give ourselves the opportunity to have an impact on the day ahead. Making an effort to greet people, taking someone a coffee or tea during the morning or acknowledging a colleague for a recent accomplishment are all simple ways to help staff be more productive and positive.

As well as observing others, consider the way *you* walk from the carpark to your office. As a leader, you are always being watched and you start transmitting your message from the moment you get out of your car. A wonderful leader I worked with for many years encouraged me to take a deep breath and pause for a second before I left my office and walked out into the 'spotlight', aka the school grounds.

"Someone is always watching," he would say, "so show them poise and control."

When you are aware of your outward appearance, even if your mind is full of the endless tasks a leader faces, you reassure your staff, parents and students that all is under control.

HINT 2: READ BODY LANGUAGE

As we master our ability to truly listen, we can begin to read the body language of the people with whom we are engaging. Is there frustration in their voice? Are they speaking too quickly or at an elevated level? Are they gesturing as they talk?

These are all indicators that the topic of conversation is not a minor issue in their mind. They may have been harbouring their thoughts for some time and have finally conjured up the courage to raise them. Even if we do not see the issue as being of great importance, it is crucial to read the signs and offer reassurance that something will be done. Remember to thank them for speaking up. Validate their concerns by saying "I appreciate you telling me this" or "Thank you for raising this issue. I see it is very important to you".

HINT 3: AVOID DEFENSIVENESS

Great leaders do not get defensive

As concerns are raised, we want to avoid becoming defensive. We must be aware of *our* body language and *our* response tone. Cutting people off with justifications or answers may only exacerbate the problem and before we know it, a verbal war has broken out and our leadership is in question. Not only do we fail to validate concerns when we become defensive, this reaction leads to dissatisfaction and encourages people to search for further issues.

Remember that people will talk and will want to bring others onside, paving the way for potential damage to the culture you are trying to establish. In most cases, an immediate answer is not essential but validation and respect are expected. Give yourself time to process the issue and make sure you respond in a timely fashion.

HINT 4: BE PROACTIVE

Be proactive not reactive to stressful situations

As leaders, we are aware of how our school operates and the different demands placed on staff at particular times of the year. Parent/teacher interviews, school concerts, camps and assessment and reporting weeks are just a few examples of when school life gets hectic. It is essential we are conscious of these periods ahead of time and do all we can to relieve any associated stress.

There are many simple ways you can do this, including:

- supplying morning tea
- bringing the coffee van in
- creating additional release time
- covering some playground duties
- allowing leeway with deadlines where possible.

At peak periods, these simple gestures affirm our teachers and show support and care. By helping staff get through these times, you will make a significant impact on their welfare which, in turn, will filter down to your students.

We cannot control everything but we do have the ability to pre-empt stressful times and do something to relieve the pressure.

HINT 5: GET TO KNOW YOUR STAFF

A high level of Emotional Intelligence will help you get the best out of others

Obviously, we are not going to pry into personal lives or stalk our staff on social media but we do need to gain an understanding of life events that may be impacting mental and emotional states. Death or illness in the family, wedding preparations, trying to fall pregnant, financial strains, marriage breakup, moving to a new house and difficulties with our own children are just a few momentous events that may affect our work lives. It is impossible to truly separate our personal life from our work life. If we want to encourage the best possible performance in the workplace, it is our responsibility as leaders to ensure adequate support is offered during challenging times.

Work-Life Fulfilment is better than Work-Life Balance

It is this elevated level of emotional intelligence that allows us to get the very best out of others. Empowering and supporting others to be the best they can be is the crux of effective leadership. Getting to know our staff, both personally and professionally, allows us to help them find work-life fulfilment and satisfaction.

Our emotional intelligence is a critical element of our development as leaders. We need to be aware of our strengths and weaknesses in this area and work on the areas of deficiency.

OVER TO YOU

EMOTIONAL INTELLIGENCE

Your emotional intelligence is your ability to read situations. It is about being mindful of your own body language and that of others and making appropriate choices based on this. We don't want to speak or react too quickly. We need poise to ensure situations are not made worse by our lack of EQ.

Watching the way others walk, *listening* to their tone, being *proactive* rather than defensive and getting to *know your staff* well are all tangible actions that will assist you in developing your emotional intelligence.

Regularly take a moment to reflect on some of the following questions.

- How well do you read people and situations?
- Does it come naturally?
- Is it an area you could develop further?
- What will you try to do to improve your emotional intelligence?
- Do you have a trusted friend or colleague who can help you be aware of the emotions you show?

CHAPTER FOUR

AFFIRM

Being in leadership sometimes forces us to focus on the problems, mistakes and issues. We are under pressure to meet performance targets and are answerable to many stakeholders, including those who sit above us (supervisors, board members and directors) and those we are responsible for (staff, students and families).

Pressure and accountability can lead us to neglect to notice all the amazing things happening in our workplace. When we do get the opportunity to get away from our desk and walk around the school, it is the small negatives we notice – untidy areas, litter, off-task behaviour and even dishes in the staffroom sink.

Look for the good in others and in situations

Take a step away from the small things and actively look for the good. Go for a walk and make a deliberate and conscious effort to only notice the positives. They will be there.

Noticing the good things gives us permission to feel better. This leads to being more positive and more confident that our staff are working effectively.

Following this realisation, the next step is critical. We have two options:

- Return to our workspace with a sense of satisfaction.
- Affirm and acknowledge our staff.

Providing our colleagues with affirmation is one of the most significant actions we can take each day. Affirmations need to be genuine and specific. People see straight through praise for something trivial or for the sake of saying we have provided praise. Later on, trivial praise will be remembered and will detract from any genuine feedback we give, making it lack credibility.

If it's not genuine, forget it!

We have all experienced the supervisor who 'does the rounds', affirming groups of staff. Sure, they can tick 'affirm staff' off their list but everyone knows it is not genuine because it is routine and non-specific. It is the same as 'every child must receive an award at assembly on Friday'. If it's not genuine, forget it.

People are motivated by intrinsic measures and extrinsic measures. The levels of motivation vary from person to person but genuine affirmation from others, especially a manager or superior, does provide the level of extrinsic motivation needed to move forward.

As educators, we understand the importance of giving behaviour-specific feedback to children. In the same way, feedback to adults will hold more value if it is linked to specific tasks or actions. Working long hours, producing impressive results, exceeding expectations or leading initiatives are among the obvious actions warranting affirmation.

I encourage you to look for the less obvious actions, too.

The more you actively observe the behaviours of your staff and their interactions with each other, the more obvious these will become.

Think about the people who routinely receive public recognition. I recall coaches of certain sports frequently receiving accolades at assembly for the recent success of their teams and the choir leader receiving awards for recent recital wins. This is not to say these events are not worthy of praise, however, there are many other moments in a school that are far less obvious but definitely affirmation-worthy.

Are you affirming the staff members that positively impact others?

For example, consider the staff member who is always smiling and positive, consistently providing encouragement to others and always helping their colleagues. This person should be affirmed for these actions because they have a great deal of influence over the climate of the school. Successful schools need these people and leaders need to notice these behaviours and value them as essential contributions.

Affirming is simple.

> *You have such a positive impact on others and I really value what you bring to our organisation.*

> *I've noticed you supporting Mary this week and it's really appreciated.*

Feedback and affirmation like this is simple to deliver and highly effective. It is specific, brief and timely. We can sometimes become so concerned with results, targets, grades and enrolments that we forget to acknowledge one of the most important aspects of our workplace – the positive influence people have on others.

Think back to your vision that encapsulates the culture you are attempting to establish. If you have staff members who behave in ways that support this culture, affirm them for it. Think about the impact certain staff members have on others. Some would come to mind as having a positive impact and others a detrimental one. These influences are powerful. Affirm those who help create the atmosphere you want and challenge the ones who impede it.

Leadership can often be lonely, which is why it is also important to affirm other leaders within your organisation. Lead by example and encourage your leader colleagues to affirm the people they work with. Make sure they know they are valued by you and speak with them about the power of positive dialogue with others.

PUBLIC OR PRIVATE?

Your level of emotional intelligence and how well you know your staff will help you determine whether public or private affirmation is best. A one-size-fits-all model will not work.

Public praising can often do more harm than good. The staff member being praised may feel uncomfortable with the attention, while others may feel left out.

At other times, public affirmation is warranted and appreciated. You need to work out which is which.

A simple rule of thumb I follow is:

- *Public affirmation for group, team or collective effort and achievements.*
- *Private affirmation for individual successes.*

Again, it comes down to knowing your staff and trusting your feelings.

OVER TO YOU

AFFIRM

Looking for the good in others and affirming this is an important aspect of leadership. The key messages are to ensure you are **genuine**. Affirmation for the sake of it or affirmation for trivial matters may be seen as tokenistic and you may lose credibility for the important affirmations. Consider whether **public** praise or **private** praise is best. You will need to know your staff well and determine which they would react to best. Look for the **less** obvious things.

Take a moment to reflect on your staff.

- How do you currently go about affirming your team?
- How could you affirm them differently?
- Is your norm to affirm the obvious successes rather than the less obvious?
- How might you improve the way your staff are recognised for the impact they have on others?

CHAPTER FIVE

DELIVER

Leaders are expected to get results. One of the reasons you chose to be a leader, and one of the reasons you were or will be selected for a leadership role, is that you get satisfaction from achieving results.

Of course, a leadership role is far more complex than this and your journey to get results will constantly change. I have met many people who 'talk the talk' and hold themselves in high regard for all they promise. Unfortunately, it is a huge letdown when leaders under-deliver and when this pattern continues their integrity is slowly but surely lost. If they do happen to make good on a promise, it is treated with surprise and some level of scepticism.

Under-promise, over-deliver

Leaders who under-promise and over-deliver quickly gain respect as being achievers. The respect of your staff is a very important step towards attaining the outcomes you are striving for. You simply cannot afford to continually let staff down by promising more than you can deliver.

By now, you will have noticed the connection between what I am saying here and what we talked about in Chapter 2 where you were encouraged to improve your listening abilities by validating the concerns of others and giving yourself time to process the information before commenting.

If someone brings a concern to you, it's a natural instinct to save the situation by promising something. The person may be immediately content but if you don't deliver, you will let them down. Try not to offer a 'quick fix' promise to resolve the problem as you are likely to forget thanks to the hundred other things going on in your day. Instead, promise you will think about it, investigate it and get back to them. Immediately make a note of your commitment. You are not promising a solution and you are giving yourself time, so you are more likely to deliver.

There is no argument against a key skill of an effective leader being a strong organisational ability. As a leader, your workload will be diverse and complex. It will often require you to deal with multiple people and multiple situations at one time. Being organised will help you deliver.

Create a system to ensure you don't neglect or forget issues and concerns that have been brought to your attention. This system needs to work for you and, most importantly, allow you to remember the promises you have made and inform the stakeholders of the decisions, results and changes you have delivered. This 'system' may be in the form of a diary, an online calendar or an email reminder tool.

UNDER-PROMISE AND OVER-DELIVER

Promises and delivery are all about perception.

For example, let's say that you receive a teacher's reports on Monday. You are confident you can have them checked by Thursday.

One option is to say you will have them back to the teacher by Friday. This is an *under-promise*. When you do manage to get them back by Thursday, the teacher not only feels they have been given an extra day to make edits but they also feel you prioritised their needs.

The emotions that emerge from this option are happy, genuine and valued.

Another option is to promise to return the reports by Wednesday. This is an *over-promise*. You still return them to the teacher by Thursday but the results are quite different even though you are returning the reports on the same day in both options. The teacher will feel let down and believe their needs were not important to you. They will probably also feel that *your* tardiness has put them behind.

Same result – different perception.

As mentioned in the opening chapter, you need your team of people to understand and own the vision you have set. You cannot get there on your own but for your staff to be supportive of your decisions, you need to gain their respect. There are many actions that will establish respect and an important one is to deliver on promises made.

Respect is mutual. You need to show respect for your colleagues if you want any chance of them respecting you. Resentment and opposition will be the result if you act like you know everything and imply it is only your opinion that matters because you wear the leadership badge.

Your ego stays at the door.

Keep an eye on your vision and remember you cannot get there without your staff. Colleagues who hold you in high regard will help you but you must give people the respect they deserve to gain the respect you desire.

Effective leaders remember the core of influence – determine your effectiveness based on the impact you have on others. A beneficial mantra is to take a little more of the blame and a little less of the credit. Chapter 9 will explore this further.

OVER TO YOU

DELIVER

One of the most important aspects for a leader to develop is their ability to get done what they say they will get done. We all appreciate leaders who are kind, friendly, present and relational, however, at the end of the day, we need to know they are achieving results.

It's easy to talk the talk. It's also easier to keep the peace by over-promising but you'll lose your credibility if you repeatedly fail to follow through with your promises.

Under-promise and over-deliver. Not only will under-promising buy you some time to take the right course of action but it will also give others confidence in your leadership.

Think about how you deliver as you consider the following questions.

- Are you a fixer?
- Have you been known to over-promise to keep the peace? (I know I have made this mistake many times.)
- Next time someone on your staff approaches you with a concern, how will you respond?
- How will you ensure you 'under-promise and over-deliver'?
- What system will you use to ensure you get back to people in a timely manner?

CHAPTER SIX

EVERYONE

Why 'everyone'? Surely we can't all be leaders?

We can.

I truly believe there is leadership potential and leadership qualities within everyone, regardless of their position. I often hear teachers say they do not want to get into leadership. I challenge this as I believe the nature of the teaching role requires the qualities of a leader. Therefore, teachers are in leadership!

Many other organisations will be the same. When staff say, "I don't want to be in leadership", they are often confusing this with administration. There may be aspects of administration and management within a leadership role but that is not what leadership entails. Any staff member who interacts with others is leading. Leadership is about influence and impact.

Leadership is defined by actions, not by position

Conversely, I sometimes see people in leadership roles who don't display the true qualities of a leader. In such cases, one could argue they are in fact not leaders. The difficulty arises when the leadership role gives people power and, by association, control over certain decisions that need to be made. Getting the right person in the leadership role is critical. It needs to be a balance *between* skill set and experience, not one or the other.

HOW DOES EVERYONE HAVE THE CAPACITY TO BE AN EFFECTIVE LEADER?

Leadership is essentially about getting the best out of others by influencing their development and performance. You can do this from any position. The way you act, interact with others, set standards, model behaviour and affirm others are all good measures of your leadership ability, regardless of your role.

Creating a competitive culture within your organisation is dangerous

If you are currently in a leadership role and refining your strengths as a leader, I urge you to look for these qualities in others. Rather than being threatened by staff members who show leadership qualities, embrace the opportunity to continue to have a positive influence on their leadership development.

Some organisations can create such a culture of internal competitiveness that it actually prevents this kind of support. Try to avoid measures within your school that encourage competitiveness among your team. Competition can cause staff to turn on each other and not provide the support and positive drive we all need to do our jobs even better. Everyone suffers.

Be aware of your staff climate. If you see cracks appearing, act fast. Discontentment at any level should be addressed professionally, respectfully and privately to ensure everyone's integrity is maintained.

Always be aware of the emotions of others and treat difficult circumstances with care

A classic example of the potential for discontentment is the internal promotion of a staff member when several internal applicants were involved.

These matters should be treated very delicately. Ultimately, you want everyone involved to still feel valued but you also need the successful applicant to receive the respect and support they deserve. As a leader, it is your responsibility to talk openly with the successful applicant and ensure they have the capacity to deal with this sensitive situation. It is important they act humbly and have insight into the emotions the unsuccessful applicants may be experiencing.

You also need to speak with the unsuccessful applicants. Validate their disappointment, affirm them and make a plan for their future. Staff who continue to apply for promotions or strive to better themselves bring motivation and strength to your school.

We need to avoid the level of disappointment that discourages people from aiming for their goals. Instead, our focus should be on helping staff plan for the future, advising on areas where they can develop and encouraging them to keep aiming high. This approach will be of great benefit to your staff and to your school as a whole.

Different people will experience varying levels of disappointment. Allowing individuals the time to process the decision is important but you must clearly state what is expected of them, particularly in relation to staff interactions.

You will utilise all your leadership qualities in addressing these types of situations. When done well, it will make a significant impact on the culture you are building. If dealt with poorly, the consequences can be catastrophic.

Publicly acknowledging staff members is another area that requires considerable thought. For public accolades to be well received, a culture of support and collegiality should be established first. If you believe a public acknowledgement could have an adverse effect and cause friction between staff, best to avoid this. Affirm privately or in a smaller, safer forum. Continue to aim for the supportive culture you require and avoid any actions that may bring harm to the achievement of your goals.

Your school will be successful if you help develop leadership qualities in your entire staff. To support and develop the capacities of everyone within your organisation, you must lead by example and be willing to share your knowledge and skills with your colleagues.

Good delegation involves clear communication of the expected outcome

Take opportunities to delegate responsibilities to your staff – not to lighten your load but to empower others.

Good delegation involves clear communication of the expected outcome and a high level of support along the way. At the same time, you need to allow people to take some ownership in achieving the goals you have set. If you prescribe every minor detail and look over their shoulder the whole way, you are not only creating more work for yourself but you are also micro-managing. The outcomes will be poor for all involved.

Scaffold for success

Be clear about your expectations and the required outcome but allow staff to make their own decisions about how they approach the task. If you are supporting them, you will have provided the necessary training before delegating. Then you will periodically check on their progress and offer encouragement or advice. Ultimately, however, you should trust your staff to own the task. This is what good delegation looks like. Scaffolding for success helps others achieve positive results and your school will benefit.

Schools are busy places. It is easy to fall into the trap of constantly delegating to the same group of people – the ones who get things done and have proved themselves as achievers. They are often also the ones who don't say no.

If we start to look for the best in all staff members and explore the leadership potential in everyone, we can begin to share the delegated tasks. This not only lightens each individual's load but also sets many staff up for successful experiences and growth within themselves.

Highly effective leaders are able to look at the strengths of each individual and offer opportunities they may not otherwise seek. Looking for the best in everyone and harnessing each person's qualities and skills will strengthen the collective efficacy of your school.

OVER TO YOU

EVERYONE

The strength of your department, faculty or school can be a direct result of how you **empower** others and get the best out of them. Looking for individual and collective strengths, building capacity and using this to enhance your team takes extraordinary leadership.

Diversity will bring vigour to your team and the benefits are endless. **Delegate** with clarity and **scaffold** for success.

Remember to look for the leadership potential in everyone as you take a moment to consider your staff and reflect on the following questions.

- Who do you notice demonstrating leadership qualities through their influence over others and how will you recognise them?
- Do you delegate enough?
- Do you delegate to different people?
- How can you support and develop the leadership potential in others?

CHAPTER SEVEN

RELATIONSHIPS

Positive relationships take time and effort to develop. We need to initiate relationship development and work to build a positive climate. Many attributes discussed in this book, such as listening, affirming and understanding the needs of others, will support relationship development. It is also important to maintain professional integrity when building relationships.

Here are a few practical suggestions for building relationships within your team.

Be fair and transparent

HINT 1: BE FAIR WITH EVERYONE

Don't treat people differently because you like one person more than another. Favouritism is very dangerous in the workplace and guaranteed to be noticed. Show fairness and equity to all by being consistent with your decisions and having justifiable reasons for them. It is important to be aware of the perception of favouritism. You may believe your close friendships with some will not hinder or affect your decisions and while this may be true, it is the perception of favouritism that will do damage.

HINT 2: TAKE CARE NOT TO DAMAGE RELATIONSHIPS

Avoid damaging your relationships as they can be difficult to repair

There will be times when a staff member makes a mistake. As the leader, you must deal with this but be sure to focus on addressing the mistake or issue, not the person.

If you attack the integrity of a staff member, you will harm your relationship with them. Damage like this is difficult to repair. You can be firm and express disapproval of the issue without getting personal or being disrespectful to the people involved.

Once the issue is dealt with, let it go. Do not harbour resentment or dwell on it and never bring it up at a later time when it is not relevant. You need to maintain the trust of your employees by showing them they are still valued in terms of their role and your relationship and that you have forgiven the error.

HINT 3: MAINTAIN A PROFESSIONAL DISTANCE

As a leader, it can be inappropriate to socialise privately with members of your staff. This can be difficult because you want to develop a relationship with them but the lines are easily crossed. You need to make a call on this and determine where those lines are.

Remember to protect your integrity as a leader as there will be times when you need to say no to a work-related request and a personal relationship with a staff member may make this difficult for you. Perception is someone else's reality. Although you may believe you are not treating one person differently, having an obvious close personal relationship with one member of staff may create the illusion of favouritism, which can be just as harmful.

HINT 4: BE OPEN AND TRANSPARENT

You want to be seen as a leader who is approachable and supportive. Your staff members need to trust you and be confident approaching you about areas of concern or with requests. If you have developed an open relationship based on trust, staff are more likely to come to you for assistance as they know their issues will be validated and their relationship with you won't be compromised. Many conversations need to be confidential or your integrity will be lost and your working relationship will suffer.

HINT 5: WORK ON DEVELOPING RELATIONSHIPS WITH EVERYONE

Developing relationships takes time but it's worth the investment.

It is important to allocate time to build relationships, especially with 'difficult' staff members.

Some people are naturally personable and easy to get along with, but others appear more distant. It is the latter with whom you need to work harder to establish and maintain a positive working relationship. They probably have a lot to offer your school, so it is essential you do not ignore them.

You are only as strong as your weakest player.

Using the above coaching analogy helps us work with everyone on staff. Good leaders will work on the difficult relationships the most and aim to get the best out of everyone.

Different stages of the relationship require different things.

ESTABLISHING THE RELATIONSHIP

The first time you meet a new staff member, smile, remember their name, listen to their initial introductions, ask them some questions about themselves and take an interest.

DEVELOPING THE RELATIONSHIP

This happens throughout the course of your relationship. Remembering something a staff member told you about and mentioning it in your conversation, delivering on a promise, getting back to people regarding a question – little things like these all help develop a relationship because they show you care.

MAINTAINING THE RELATIONSHIP

This is perhaps the most challenging stage. The key is trust. Ensure your integrity remains intact, never talk about staff members to others and maintain confidences. Trust is easily broken but takes a long time to repair.

OVER TO YOU

RELATIONSHIPS

Relationships with staff, parents, students, colleagues and other stakeholders need to be nurtured. Once **established**, they must be **developed** and **maintained**. Being fair, honest and transparent, and showing integrity are the keys to maintaining these relationships.

Challenging conversations are likely to be far more productive when you have formed relationships based on trust. It is essential to continue to work on relationships with everyone – especially those relationships that are more difficult.

Regularly reflect on your professional relationships.

- What are your workplace relationships like?
- Does your opinion of these relationships match the perception?
- Identify any relationships that need repairing and make a plan to start.
- What can you do to remember people's names? (It's more important than we realise.)
- How can you lead the development of better relationships among your whole staff?

CHAPTER EIGHT

SUPPORT

Part of the culture you should be aiming to develop must include a supportive environment for your staff. Everything you put in place needs to reflect this. There are a few simple and effective ways you can achieve a supportive environment.

HINT 1: CLEAR POLICIES AND PROCEDURES

If your policies and procedures are well-documented and known by staff, they will help create a supportive environment. Wherever possible, involve your staff in the policy development process to ensure shared ownership. You may utilise the skills of a focus group or task force to develop the draft policy but there should also be opportunities for all staff to provide feedback or have input into the policy.

Policies and procedures, such as grievance procedures, communication policies and code of conduct policies, are critical. If staff are involved in their development and review, they are more likely to adhere to them.

Referring to them regularly and ensuring they are accessible and all staff abide by them will benefit your school.

If, for example, the communication policy states that teachers will not respond to school emails after a certain time in the evening, then all staff must support each other by abiding by this. As soon as one teacher acts outside of this policy, perhaps by emailing a parent late at night, it sets up an expectation from parents that all teachers will do so. When those following the communication policy respond the next day, parents may be disgruntled and feel they are not being treated seriously. These policies need to be clearly communicated with parents and staff to reinforce expected behaviour and continue to build effective relationships with everyone involved in the school community. If we don't support and act within the agreed policies, procedures and guidelines, we can set our colleagues up.

HINT 2: FOCUS ON BEING EFFECTIVE

Efficiency is good but effectiveness is better.

Empowering your staff to solve problems themselves will save you time in the long run. Spend time with your staff, offer your support and build their capacity.

Consider how you support teams, not just individuals

HINT 3: SUPPORT TEAMS

Supporting individual staff members is essential but so is team support. The collective expertise of your staff, if supported, will drive your school further. By nature, people like to feel connected to others and a shared project, vision or task can provide this. Support the team to achieve results and lead positively by providing direction, assistance, resources and time. Take a genuine interest in their work. Be mindful, however, that you do not take over.

HINT 4: DEVELOP MENTORING AND INDUCTION PROGRAMS FOR ALL STAFF

By implementing mentoring and induction programs, you are supporting the leadership qualities in other staff as they manage these initiatives. If you are serious about aiming for a supportive culture, you need to develop processes at multiple levels and involve many people. Recognising and nurturing the leadership qualities in your staff is an important step towards achieving this goal.

Explore the key elements of change and the associated emotions, as depicted in the following matrix.

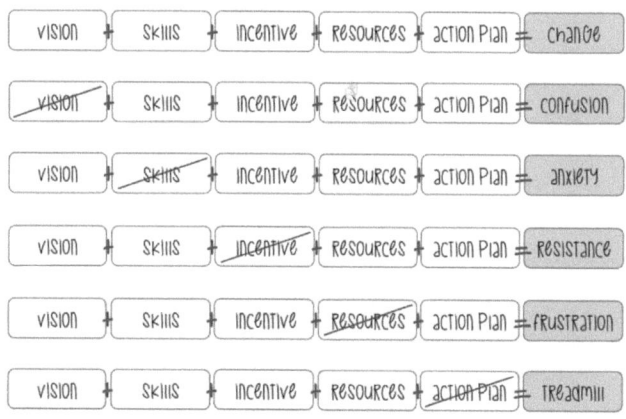

It is important to remember the emotion listed on the far right is not your emotion but the one demonstrated by the people you are aiming to influence. For example, in the second row, an unclear vision leads to confusion. In the fifth row, a lack of required resources, including time, leads to frustration.

Look for the emotions in others to help determine your actions

Consider the emotions you are seeing in your staff or team. If they are displaying one of the emotions on the right, you need to provide the missing link. For example, if you notice resistance, your job as the leader is to help your staff find an incentive. If you see anxiety, your role is to provide skills development.

Your emotional intelligence will help you identify and interpret these emotions. From there, you can work out where the problem lies and how to address it.

As a leader, it is important to recognise the emotions you are seeing in others. Remember, you can steer the boat but if no one is paddling you won't get far.

OVER TO YOU

SUPPORT

Supporting your staff, both individually and as a group, will help everyone in your school achieve. There will be times when people thrive and times when they need to be propped up. Leaders need to be there when additional support is required as well as when things are running smoothly. If you don't step up when your staff need you the most, your absence will be felt. And it will be remembered. Keep looking for avenues to support every team member to be successful and celebrate their achievements with them.

The ability to reflect is one of the most powerful attributes you have. Use it regularly to read and interpret the emotions of your staff.

- When have you seen members of your staff display any or all of the emotions listed on the matrix? Delve deeper into one of these instances.
- What was your role in creating this emotion?
- How did you respond and, more importantly, what could you have done differently?

CHAPTER NINE

HUMILITY

 How many times a day do you say the word 'I'? Being humble, despite all your achievements, is one of the truly great characteristics of effective leaders. Look at some of the significant leaders we have seen over the years: Mahatma Gandhi, Barack Obama, Nelson Mandela, Fred Hollows, Eddie Mabo.

Great leaders show incredible humility

As leaders, these people showed incredible humility. They led for the betterment of others rather than their own rise to greatness. In *Wisdom's Way* (2013), Trinidad Hunt speaks about success versus significance through her wonderful, leadership-themed poetry. She explains that the heart of a true leader knows the difference between success and significance. Having already achieved success, they aim for significance.

There are appropriate 'networks' for you to bask in your own glory – close family and friends perhaps. As for your colleagues and staff, they certainly do not want to hear how wonderful you believe you and your achievements are. Your actions will gain their respect, not your narrative.

When achievements are made, ensure others receive the glory rather than you. When mistakes are made, take your share of the blame plus a little extra for good measure.

I often see leaders in schools who shoulder the busiest workloads. This may well apply to you but no one wants to hear how busy you are. Imagine your reaction if your first Principal or Deputy Principal flopped down at the staffroom table with a sigh, exclaiming, "I'm so busy." I doubt your first thought would be: Wow, you must be an extraordinary leader – I'm so impressed by you and what you do. I know mine wouldn't.

Instead, I would be thinking something like: they earn the big money. Or I'd be wondering why they don't delegate instead of doing it all. I may even start to think they didn't trust the staff to handle the responsibility.

Earlier in this book, I discussed the power of effective leadership in terms of influence – the impact and effect you have on others. Humility is a true leadership characteristic and has a powerful and long-lasting impact on others. You need to ensure you have the self-confidence to believe you are leading well, without regularly needing to be told you are by others.

The staffroom is not the place for self-promotion

Self-promotion is an important skill to have. Applying for a job, for example, requires the ability to promote yourself. Many people, particularly women, tend to talk themselves out of applying for a position if they don't feel they meet **all** the necessary requirements of the role. In these instances, too much humility can be detrimental. Be mindful of showcasing your abilities in these situations.

Of course, in other spaces, self-promotion should really be kept to a minimum. Constantly talking about all your achievements and how wonderful you are – the 'me-show' – will make you unpopular in the staffroom. This is when self-promotion turns into bragging.

OVER TO YOU

HUMILITY

Humility is remembering that your success is not solely about you – it's about your team. True humility means taking less of the credit for yourself and celebrating your team's success instead.

If you ever need a concrete example of this, listen to Australian tennis player, Ash Barty, when she accepts awards in post-match interviews. She continually mentions 'her team', largely avoids or diverts individual accolades and refers only to the people surrounding her. This is genuine humility.

Take time now to reflect on your own humility.

- Are you humble?
- Would those you lead say you are humble?
- What is it like to be led by you?
- Do you have a safe place to acknowledge your achievements?
- Do the leaders around you show humility?
- How can you ensure you practise humility and support others to do so as well?

CHAPTER 10

INTEGRITY

Integrity is a word we often tend to throw around when we talk about leadership. It's a value most of us would agree we admire. But what exactly is integrity?

The Macquarie Online Dictionary defines integrity as follows:

noun 1. soundness of moral principle and character; uprightness; honesty.

What this means is that you show integrity when you respect the opinions of others, address conflict honestly, take responsibility for your actions and errors and act as a role model.

With this in mind, there is a clear interconnection between honesty and trust – so let's talk about trust for a moment.

The underlying foundation of any positive culture is trust. Colleagues trust each other, leaders trust each other, colleagues trust leaders and leaders trust colleagues. We have each other's back.

Trust is a powerful commodity for all leaders

There are several factors that help create trust but a key one is consistency. For your staff to trust you, they need to feel like they know what your actions will be. This comes about through consistency of behaviour.

If a leader always has the children's best interests at the core of the decision-making process, and this never wavers, it allows a level of trust to be developed. The consistency of the leader's behaviour means staff will not worry they might be blindsided by a decision. Staff will feel confident to trust their leader's decision-making as all past decisions have demonstrated integrity through consistency. When leaders show consistency, asking for something should feel relatively safe. In fact, you are likely to already know the answer before you ask.

When there is no consistency, your staff will begin to feel less safe and more confused. The fear of asking something if the response could be one of many can lead to anxiety.

HOW DO WE BUILD AND MAINTAIN TRUST?

Schools want leaders who are trustworthy. When you demonstrate integrity, you show everyone you can be trusted. Integrity requires a firm adherence to a code of moral or artistic values.

I worked with an exceptional leader while in the role of Assistant Principal at a large South Australian college. This leader lived integrity – not only through his words but through the consistency of his actions. He always encouraged differences of opinion and provided safe places to speak your mind.

He believed we were a stronger team due to our diversity. Our mantra was: we don't have to agree but we must align. Once debate had occurred, he would ask, "How will our decisions impact the students?" This was his moral compass and whether I agreed with his final decision or not, I was always accepting and supportive of it because of his integrity. I trusted him.

Developing and nurturing trust is where the power of integrity comes in. Chapter 7 touched on this when relationships were explored but we will now look a little deeper into this concept.

The first thing to remember is to be very clear about your vision and what drives it. Throughout this book, you have been encouraged to consider the question: What is it like to be led by me? We have explored a number of attributes of effective leadership with the aim of developing a clear picture of the leader you are and the leader you want to become.

When you are clear about your leadership style and you understand what drives you, decisions become easier. Further to this, when you make integral decisions and can articulate why, it is far easier for everyone to align.

Integrity is not doing what is easy, it is doing what is right

Your integrity is built around the reasons behind your decisions, regardless of the consequences. You are not doing what is easy. You are doing what you believe is right.

Trust starts with truth and ends with truth.

~ Santosh Kalwar ~

When you have integrity, your values, decisions and actions become more consistent and your staff will begin to trust you.

You cannot live by values if you do not know what you truly believe in.

Start by defining your core values. These are the values you will not compromise on, no matter what the consequences are.

At the beginning of this book, you were asked to choose a leader you admire. Think about them again for a moment and the reasons you admire them. Maybe they demonstrate integrity? Perhaps they are consistent? Or did they build trust among the staff?

OVER TO YOU

INTEGRITY

When your moral compass is in check because you have clearly defined values, all your decisions will be consistent – even the tough ones.

Consistency leads to **trust** and demonstrates your **integrity**.

Your team may not always agree with your decisions but they are more likely to accept them if there is a clear understanding regarding **why** you made them in the first place. Your 'why' is governed by your integrity.

Think about yourself and your actions and discuss the following questions with a mentor or another leader.

- How do you show integrity?
- What was a time your decision was made easier because you were clear about your values and your integrity was in check?
- How might you improve this area of your leadership?

CHAPTER ELEVEN

PRESENCE

What is your presence as a leader?

Presence is a powerful characteristic and is dependent on the perception of others. Your presence may not be as important as some of the other qualities and attributes we have discussed but it does have an impact on how your school community behaves.

The confidence people have in you is determined by your presence. Your presence can also intimidate. It can encourage open lines of communication. It can drive conversation underground.

Your presence is significant.

Be deliberate about your presence

Think not only about the presence you believe you have as a leader but also of the presence you want to have. It has to be deliberate and needs to be considered.

Do you present as meek, mild, quiet and unseen? Or are you loud, aggressive, intimidating and demanding?

Do you appear confident, controlled and poised? Or are you erratic, reactive and scatty?

Very early in my leadership journey, I was told:

Do not apologise for leading. Lead with passion and conviction. You will make mistakes. Own them. Be proud to lead.

As someone who likes to please others and not 'rock the boat', these words stuck with me. There were times I had to make tough decisions. Remembering this advice gave me courage to develop my presence as a leader.

You will be influenced by leaders you admire and the presence they have and, from this, you will develop your own presence. Remember, in leadership, someone is always watching. Take a deep breath before you leave the privacy of your office then walk around your school with poise and purpose.

Consider your leadership in the classroom. Your students will see if you are rushed, frantic and overwhelmed. They will become unsettled and restless. However, calm and controlled actions relax our students and allow them to refocus.

Leadership with adults is the same. As the leader, if you are flustered, your staff will not only notice this but it will very likely filter down to the students. If you are poised, confident and measured, this will also influence the behaviour and presence of your staff and positively impact the experiences of your students.

I have worked with some incredible leaders and watched how they built trust, worked with poise and empowered me and other members of the team. I have also worked with many leaders who were not able to develop this presence. What's important is the learning that came about from both. Being reflective of your own presence by learning from others is a powerful advantage. You are you. You need to be authentic as you create your presence and stand firm for what you believe in. Learn from others, both good and bad, and develop your self-confidence to be an admirable leader – one you would follow and one you believe in.

There is no 'right' way to lead and leaders certainly come in all shapes and sizes. If we continue to accept that we are not perfect, growth will happen. Be a better leader today than you were yesterday and be a better leader tomorrow than you are today. This mindset will allow you to do incredible things and genuinely make a difference in the lives of others.

OVER TO YOU

PRESENCE

What is it like to be led by you?

How do others see you as a leader?

Your presence is vital and you are the only person who can determine how you are seen. Do you want to be seen as strong, bold and decisive? Perhaps you want people to see you as confident, hard-working and efficient? Maybe you see yourself as relational, kind and supportive? Of course, you may be a combination of all of these – this is for you to consider but remember there will always be someone watching.

Be proud to lead and passionate about your role. Have confidence in yourself and become the leader you would follow.

Take time to reflect on the following, thinking about how others may see you.

- Consider your body language and facial expressions during public events, such as assemblies and meetings. Do you express a welcoming and open manner or does your body language create tension?
- What messages do you think are portrayed by your presence? Are there any that need to change or need to be amplified?
- Do you need to develop your presence further? Have you considered filming yourself when you speak publicly?

- Do you have someone you trust who can give you honest feedback about your current presence?

CHAPTER TWELVE

THE BEST LEADER YOU CAN BE

The LEADERSHIP acronym detailed throughout this book is a simple approach you can take to develop your self-mastery as a leader and have a greater impact and influence on others. While there are many facets to leadership – the ability to manage projects, organise events and budget wisely, to name a few – the true simplicity of leadership is about the influence you have on others.

The ten elements that make up LEADERSHIP are an easy place to start. You have complete control over how much time and energy you place on the development of each element and on how well you perform.

We can always improve and strive for more. Your ability to reflect on your impact will positively affirm your leadership drive and will help you adjust when required. Self-reflection is powerful.

As your leadership journey continues, your reflections throughout this book will help you fulfil your dream of becoming the best leader you can be.

Challenges will continue to be thrown your way but each situation will be unique and offer you opportunities to strive for new goals.

Our impact and influence on others is what leadership is all about. We can only control our own behaviours – not the behaviours of others. However, we can certainly influence behaviours by what we stand for, how we interact and how we lead.

Whether you're an aspiring leader, in your first leadership role or have a decade of leadership experience – you are always going to need to make time for reflection.

After you've faced each new situation or dealt with a challenging issue, take time to breathe and think.

- Did things go to plan?
- How could I have handled that differently?
- Would the outcome have changed?
- Did my actions align with my beliefs?
- What will I do next time?
- What areas of my leadership can I continue to improve?
- Who can support me?

Start building your capacity in the ten areas discussed throughout this book. They are reproduced on the next page as a handy reference.

OVER TO YOU

THE ACRONYM SUMMARISED

L Listen (don't fix)

E Emotional intelligence (reflect before you react)

A Affirm (be genuine)

D Deliver (under-promise, over-deliver)

E Everyone (look for and empower the leadership capacity in others)

R Relationships (establish, develop and maintain relationships)

S Support (teams and individuals)

H Humility (significance not success)

I Integrity (build trust)

P Presence (be the leader you would follow)

Every day, make time to reflect, revisit your goals and ask yourself:

What is it like to be led by me?

REFERENCES

Covey, Stephen R. 2004. *The 7 Habits Of Highly Effective People: Restoring The Character Ethic [Rev. Ed]*. New York: Free Press.

Hunt, D. Trinidad. 2013. *Wisdom's Way*. 1st ed. Elan Press.

Santosh Kalwar. 2010. *Quote Me Everyday*. 1st ed. Lulu Press.

Macquariedictionary.com.au. 2022. *Macquarie Dictionary*. [online] Available at: <https://www.macquariedictionary.com.au/> [Accessed 14 March 2022].

To find out more about Jodie Davey and the courses she offers through
Powerful Partnerships, visit her website
https://www.powerfulpartnerships.com.au/
or contact Jodie directly at
jodie@powerfulpartnerships.com.au

Printed by Libri Plureos GmbH in Hamburg, Germany